Project Five-Star:

The Five Points of Hope

By

I0429528

Michael Harrison Fox

Need a
Home?
Stay with
us!

Get Healthy!

Learn a skill and
use it!

**Project
Five-Star**

Find a job!

Find a new
home!

Dedicated to all homeless everywhere, who have struggled with the current shelter systems and the current economy, in hopes of making this idea a reality.

The Job's Not Done

I've been thinking lately about my life
My body hurts, the debt's piled high
I'm feeling as though the well's run dry
I turn my eyes to the skies above
And I wonder aloud 'Where's the Love?'

I get   feeling in my heart
That tells me not to worry
You've got a job to do
And you're too much in a hurry

Just look at the world around you
The world needs love around you

Refrain
The Job's Not Done
The Job's Not Done
The Job's Not Done

I took another look at my life
Take and take and take some more
Selfishness was at my core
But there comes a time for that to end
Before my heart starts to rend

That feeling in my heart
Tells me I got it all wrong

To get love you have to give
That's the way it's been all along

I looked at the world around me
Suffering and war around me

(Refrain)

I looked at other people's lives
I've seen poverty and despair
Homelessness, I want to care
But it's not an easy job to do
I need your help, all of you

My heart tells me
That these people shouldn't suffer
Let's give them hope and love
So their lives don't get any rougher

Let's look at the world around us
Just look at the world around us

Why do I go on?
Why do I go on?

(Refrain)

- Michael Harrison Fox

Table of Contents

Introduction

Project Five-Star comes from my own experiences with being homeless. I have lived in 4 different shelters over the last 20 years, homeless for a variety of reasons, all due to some shortcoming of my own.

Some shelters are better than others, as you'll see from the descriptions I'll give. Also some shelters provide better service on one day than on another. Some are consistently bad. Some aren't bad one day, but horrible the next. The overall effect of the current homeless shelter system in America, however, is to drive a man to want to get out as soon as possible, even to the point of driving him out before he is ready.

I will be most vivid in my descriptions of shelters when referring to the South Wilmington Street Center, in Raleigh, NC. As I write this book, SWSC is my home, and though better than others, it is missing some of the key factors that we, as homeless men, need the most. I do not mean to denigrate the efforts put out by Wake County or the staff of SWSC, I just wish to point out, that no matter how well the homeless are treated, it could always be better.

Part I

Why The Need?

Chapter 1

The Current Situation

My first experience with being homeless was a relatively pleasant one. I was stuck in Springfield, Massachusetts in 1990, broke, homeless and jobless. The shelter there, run by the city, I believe, had a general population that stayed in bunks on the bottom floor, and rooms in the floors above for those that had jobs and just needed time to save up money. There was food to eat, and though my memory of it is faded, I can't say it was bad.

I found a job quickly, saved some money, and then moved into a roommate situation. Not a bad first introduction to homeless shelters. However, it offered no assistance as far as job training, and resources to help me find a job and a place to live were scattered. Not the last time I would encounter this. I managed to find a job quickly enough to avoid having to apply for Food Stamps or other welfare.

Honestly, if all shelters were run like that I would have little to complain about. Alas, that was not the case. My next encounter with being homeless came in 2005, when an attempt to go into business for myself ended disastrously. Worse was a car wreck that left me with no means of transportation other than the bus and my own two feet. I wound up in Roanoke, Virginia. Roanoke is a beautiful town, but I found only two shelters there, both run by Christian agencies.

The Roanoke Rescue Mission was my first stop. I had been ill before going into it, from a stomach ulcer caused by stress. When the hospital released me, they gave me a voucher for cab fare to the Rescue Mission. It seemed like every homeless person in Roanoke went there. The daily routine, which never changed, went something like this:

At 5pm, after a day spent hunting for jobs, I'd head to the shelter to wait in line with a hundred or more other men. The shelter would open its doors and men would file in, stand in line some more while staff assigned beds, then you were given a shirt, with your bed number on it, deliberately large enough to cover your entire body. You were ordered to strip, give all your belongings to staff, and head for the shower where you and 10 other naked men were given 3 minutes to clean yourselves, and then march out to put on your shirt. Some men just pretended to take showers, getting just wet enough to seem like they tried.

The shirts were made of some material that itched and scratched your naked body. It was the only thing you were allowed to wear. The clothes you wore in were laundered and returned to you the next morning.

After showering, you were fed. Shelters in the south must think cabbage is the best vegetable a man can eat, because that's all they served. The other foods were generally barely edible. Yet some people could eat it. I remember two grossly fat men, disgusting to see in the shower, begging or coercing food from other people.

After dinner, everyone was forced into a chapel to hear a preacher tell us we were eternally damned to the fires of hell unless we repented. We sang hymns from a book of hymns dated to 1900. Mostly the same ones over and over again.

This lasted until 9pm when it was time for sleep. Anyone who has slept in a dorm situation knows the sounds men can make in their sleep. Multiply that by a hundred. Snores, farts, sneezes and a variety of other sounds and smells permeate a homeless shelter at night. If you're a light sleeper like me, it's hard to get to sleep and stay asleep.

Morning comes, or at least 5am, and you're awakened by staff. You get your freshly-laundered clothes, change and head to breakfast, in which the food is worse than dinner. Grits day after day are no way to feed a man, yet every southern shelter I've lived in seemed to relish serving it. And stale bread that no one else will eat makes a poor donation.

After leaving the shelter, comes the attempt to find a job. With no transportation and no money for the bus, I walked with my belongings, because I couldn't leave them in the shelter. I usually found myself at the library where I used their computers to search for a job online. I had no phone. I had an email address I could use in case they were interested, but they could not call me. Jobs were hard enough to come by without giving employers an excuse not to hire you. And if you did have an interview, coming in while dragging a suitcase makes an interesting first impression, doesn't it?

The library had computers and books that I read to pass the time waiting to hear from an employer. The library staff, keenly aware that many of the users there were homeless, were eager to pounce on you if you happened to doze off because you did not get enough sleep the night before. I felt unwelcome.

There were other resources in Roanoke. I finally applied for Food Stamps and received a month's worth for emergency use. I used several sources to get some clothes to replace the tattered clothes I was wearing. There is a day shelter in Roanoke, where on a cold day someone who is homeless can come to get warm and to possibly find day work. One of the men who ran it, seeing that I needed good shoes for interviews, gave me a pair, but warned me half-jokingly that he wanted a piece of my first paycheck.

And so the days passed, with no work forthcoming. The shelter started to wear on me, and I started hearing about the Salvation Army shelter in Roanoke. I checked it out. It seemed a clean, quiet place to rest my weary bones. They allowed me in, warning me that I had six weeks to find a job or I would be asked to leave.

At first the shelter seemed like paradise, especially compared to the Rescue Mission. The food was good, the beds warm and it was not as crowded. I could leave my meager belongings behind. There were rules, of course. We only had to attend church service 3 times a week, We had to work at their store twice a week. That cut into my job searching time, and I still had no phone, except that of the shelter. And what employer wants to call the phone number supplied by a potential employee to hear 'Salvation Army Men's Shelter?'

Six weeks passed, without any bite for a job. The Salvation Army kicked me out. Back to the Rescue Mission I went. Back to the dreary existence that clouded my mind, filling me with doubt about my own sanity, where so many around me had clearly lost theirs. I had a friend recently tell me of a study done in Canada where up to 70% of the homeless in shelters had mental health issues. It was obvious in the Rescue Mission that that number was no lie.

I was fast becoming one of those statistics when I got an offer for a days work, holding a sign for a furniture store holding a bankruptcy sale. I took the work, got the $50 in cash for it, and bought a bus ticket to Raleigh, North Carolina. I had done some research while in the library and found jobs aplenty there, and a decent-looking shelter system. I jumped at the chance. I will admit that what primarily drew me was their free voice mail system.

So I hopped a Greyhound Bus and made the trip to Raleigh. I arrived on a Saturday, lucky for me, tired, hungry and in need of a break. On Saturdays the South Wilmington Street Center, the shelter run by Wake County, is open all day, as well as the night. The first time you go into the center, you are guaranteed a bed. I spent some time filling out paperwork, and then ate and went to bed, exhausted.

The center is broken down into 5 dorms. All but one dorm have a series of bunk beds. The center itself holds around 240 men, and is full most nights.

Those not in program dorms have to rely on a lottery system each day to determine if they get into the shelter that night. Each morning you check the list to see what your number is. I've seen as many as 700 people on the lottery list. Only about 100 get in. The rest have to find shelter elsewhere, or sleep in the streets.

The process to get into a program dorm takes at least a week. You have to take 4 hour-long courses that cover things like money and anger management. Once you complete the courses you get placed on a waiting list, waiting for the program dorms to empty enough to make room for you. What you're really waiting for is the caseload of the case workers to lighten enough for them to handle the influx of new program guests. This implies someone has to leave in order for you to get in. This process can take several weeks depending on where you are on the waiting list.

Once you are in the program you have to pass a drug and alcohol test, then you get a secured bed for the duration of your stay.

Staying at SWSC is a mixture of experiences. On

one hand you have a place to sleep every night, and a place to put your belongings. On the other hand the staff takes no responsibility if your belongings are stolen. On one hand you get two meals a day. On the other the quality of the food, especially breakfast, varies from day to day. One day you might have chicken breasts, but they might be undercooked. You will almost certainly get cabbage, but that is overcooked. You might get an 8-ounce carton of milk at breakfast and a 4-ounce bag of orange juice or apple juice. The only way to open the bag is with your teeth. The utensils are plastic and not very durable. The whole kitchen area has a feeling of being under-funded.

Breakfast usually consists of grits, stale bread, occasionally an egg in one form or another. Sometimes they have milk. They always have that bag of juice. Sometimes the grits are substituted with oatmeal, or biscuits and gravy. Sometimes we get lucky and get very thin pancakes with syrup. On a couple of occasions they'll serve those same pancakes for dinner and in their menu board liken it to Denny's Grand Slam Breakfast. All I have to say is if Denny's served food like that they'd go out of business pretty fast.

Dinner is just a little bit better. It can range from the under-cooked chicken to a small serving of pasta and tomato sauce to something they call Jambalaya. The one consistency is their glass of watered-down Kool-Aid that often has less taste than the tasteless dinner they serve. It's watered down because they fill the glasses with ice and

Kool-Aid 45 minutes before dinner is served

I've heard it said that they rely on food donations to make the dinners there, and often church groups will come in bringing their own food. But altogether too often I've foregone dinner or breakfast because the food was entirely too unappetizing.

Other exciting things lay before me in learning to cope with the shelter. In a dorm with 40 males, snoring is just one sound that keeps you awake at night. You can sometimes hear phones ringing and people talking on their cells. This is actually against the rules of the Center and men have been kicked out - barred - for allowing that to happen. People talk in the dorms at night, even after lights out at 9pm, keeping light sleepers like myself awake. The smells of the men permeate the dorm. One of the worst sounds, however, is the sound of people walking back and forth to the bathroom or their beds. A few of them wear flip-flops and in a dorm setting, the noise is quite pervasive. And some of them aren't content with going to their beds. They go to their beds or bathroom, then walk out. Then a few minutes later they do it all over again. A few even pace in the dorm. When you're trying to get some shut-eye, it's hard to do when you're constantly interrupted.

But once you do get to sleep, embrace that sleep, because at 5:30am every morning the lights go on and you are expected to get up. Breakfast is served at roughly 5:45am, and they stop serving at 6:30. If you are in the emergency dorms, you have to be out by 7am. If you are in the program dorms, you have to be out by 8am. If you like taking showers alone, good luck! You have to share the showers with 40 other men, though not at the same time, and though it's possible to take a shower uninterrupted, reality tells you that's not easy. Some take their showers at night; some start taking showers at 4am to beat the rush.

After you shower and dress, comes the day. If you're broke, you either need to beg or borrow a bus pass from someone or walk. It's a 20 minute walk from the shelter to downtown Raleigh. Resources for a homeless man are scattered in Raleigh, just like everywhere else. The Human Services Department, where you sign up for Food Stamps, is too far to walk. So is the NC ESC, for unemployment and Job Link. Sometimes staff in the center has a bus pass to give you, but they prefer to save those for people who are interviewing.

One thing that is right in downtown Raleigh is the Soup Kitchen. I've been there sporadically, because every homeless person in town seems to come there. And some of them carry bugs with them. I hate having to stand in line for the soup kitchen with someone in front of me who is scratching, only to find myself scratching shortly afterward.

So most of my time is spent at the Wake County Public Library. They have computers to use, though usage is limited. But don't accidentally doze there, or you'll get the same treatment I received in

Roanoke. "Sir! No sleeping in the library!"

Laundry services in the shelter are limited to 5 washers and 5 dryers. As the manager of the shelter recently pointed out, these are not heavy-duty washers and dryers. With more than 240 men who use it, the washers break down often. At any given time you are lucky to see 3 working washers and an equal number of dryers that really dry. So get ready to line up for that 'free' service. And if you are in the program dorms, be prepared to bring your own detergent. Washers are frequently fought over, or argued over at least.

My first time in SWSC I was lucky enough to find a job relatively quickly. I was really lucky, though. I had set up the Community Voice Mail and sure enough, got a call for an interview. I thought I had heard the directions clearly enough, but when I got off the bus stop closest to the place, I took a wrong turn. I had a shirt, pants, tie and jacket, and it was a hot July day. I walked around a total of an hour before I finally found the place. I was hot, sweaty, thirsty and late. I had to beg the receptionist for a cup of water. The woman who interviewed me must have thought me a sight, and I thought for sure I had blown that interview. But I hadn't and the next day I got a call.

So I had finally found a job after 7 months of unemployment. Yet I could not leave the shelter just like that. I worked that job as hard as I could, and started saving money. I put up with the nightly rituals of noise and I got 'promoted' to a dorm where it was quieter and I could come and go at all hours. 'E Dorm' had no bunk-beds, but had the same flimsy mattresses as the other dorms. It was smaller than the other dorms and there were walls separating each set of two beds. At worst you had to put up with the noise of one other person. I thought I was in paradise.

And yet even that was temporary. As I earned more money, I took a required course called 'Ready to Rent,' which is provided as a means to find an apartment without having to go through their applications and other qualifying criteria. After that course, I moved into a separate building called 'IHD,' which closely resembled a boarding house, but it was still run by Wake County. IHD allowed you to have a TV and your own room, and you paid rent of $300 per month.

After a total of a year in the Wake County shelter system, I had finally saved up enough money to get my new apartment. I chose one on the bus line that sent me to work. It was a one-bedroom apartment that was comfortable for me and had affordable rent. I was finally out of the shelter.

Yet, despite that, I was still struggling financially. I had bills to pay that ate into my take-home pay and made things difficult. The Food Stamps I had received only lasted 3 months, and I was only getting by on the skin of my teeth.

And my health had suffered inside the shelter. My teeth had slowly been rotting away, and though

I had insurance, the dentist told me right up front that it would cost $10,000 to get them fixed. I left them as they were.

Later, I started to feel tired all the time, and when I went to my doctor, I discovered I had Type II Diabetes. I resolved to control it with diet and exercise, and that seemed to work at first.

But the toll of living from paycheck to paycheck was high. After 4 years of working for the same company, the company was bought out. I was kept in my same position, but I had lost my Social Security card at some point since I had originally started working for them. I was born in France, and I had to send off for a copy of my birth certificate in order to get the Social Security card replaced. The company would not wait any longer for the documents and let me go. Three days later I got the birth certificate, but they refused to rehire me.

I had managed to pay that month's rent before being let go, but I knew I had to find something quickly or I would find myself in the shelter again.

I found a job working from home, using my computer and home phone to be tech support for Sprint Smartphones. I started that at the end of August. September's rent was late, but I managed to earn enough money to barely keep up the payments, though I had to pay late fees every month.

Then Sprint cut back on the hours, and I fell further and further behind. By the time the hours started creeping up to where I could make payments, I was two months behind and threatening letters started coming from my landlord. At the end of March, 2010, I went to court, and the judge granted them an eviction.

I had two weeks to get out, and I did, taking only what I could carry and leaving many of my accumulated belongings behind. I had an idea of hiking the Appalachian Trail, and living off the land for a while, working on my writing and getting in shape. That lasted all of ten days. I came back to Raleigh exhausted, dirty and almost penniless, once again.

The shelter beckoned, and I had to go through the same process of getting into the program as the first time. The shelter had not changed at all in 5 years, but the job situation had. It was harder than ever to find a job in Raleigh. Added to that was the lack of air conditioning in the dorms. The staff blamed it on a broken part, which they had to have custom-made. It took them two of the hottest months to get it repaired.

Yet I did find another job, as a tech support person for Apple Computers. I did not work directly for Apple, though, the job was outsourced to a company called Affiliated Computer Services. The job took a month to start, and the training class ran from 6:30am until 3pm Monday through Friday for 3 weeks.

The company was located not too far from a bus

stop, but the early hours and the fact that I had a 20 minute walk from the bus stop meant I had to take an earlier bus than I liked to get there. The bus left Moore Square at 4:30am, which meant I had to get up at 3:45am to be able to shower and walk downtown to get there.

So for 3 weeks I struggled to get up every morning, after a not so good night sleep, tried to keep awake during the training class, and managed to learn how to do my job without being fired. I begged my case manager to let me stay in 'E Dorm' because it was quieter and I could come and go at all hours, but I was turned down.

After 3 weeks of training, I started working my regular schedule. I worked 12pm-9pm, which on the outset seemed like a good schedule, but between having to still get up at 5:30am and leave by 8am, and then arriving back at the shelter sometime after 11pm, I was in worse condition than before. Again I begged to be put into 'E Dorm,' and was told I could not.

I could not stand the situation any longer. Armed with a couple of weeks of pay, I moved out of the shelter and into a motel that charged by the week. It was on the bus line to where I worked and I could now get the sleep I so desperately needed.

And yet, the rent was so high that I was literally living paycheck to paycheck. I had once again started receiving Food Stamps, but when they ran out, I often found myself with no money for food for several days.

I put up with that for 7 months. Stress at work had increased exponentially and was negatively affecting my health. I left ACS after a call from a panicked woman sent me into a panic too.

But this time I had a few days and a full paycheck to work with, and I was determined to be ready to enter the shelter - for the last time. I bought a laptop computer, the same one I am typing this book into, and two months worth of bus passes. I bought a cell phone and two months of service. I had two tax refunds that would be coming my way at some point in the near future, and I was ready.

I moved back into the shelter at the end of March 2011. I worked daily at the library, both looking for jobs and writing. I submitted one of my scripts to a contest in hopes it would be noticed. I was at the library 7 days a week for the first month and a half.

The Federal Tax refund I had been expecting came back quickly, but it was also spent quickly, on one more bus pass, more time on my phone and other needed items, like socks and underwear.

Then two things happened that shattered my hopes: First my cell phone was stolen. I had laid it down at the entrance of the shelter in order to be searched. I left it on the table not 30 seconds, but by the time I came back, it was gone. Staff hadn't seen anything. They're not responsible.

Second, the next day my wallet was stolen. I had accidentally left it on the bus and when I realized it, 30 seconds too late, it was gone. The bus driver said someone else claimed it. The wallet had all my ID and two bus passes. I kept no money in the wallet. The bus passes were the worst loss for me. I would eventually replace the ID, but those two bus passes cost me $72. I was devastated.

Yet I tried to go on, walking to downtown Raleigh and catching the R Line bus took me within easy walking distance to the library. I kept looking for a job, even though I had no phone. I discovered Google Voice, a free voice mail service offered by Google. With the right equipment you could even make calls.

The contest I entered came back in a disappointing fashion. Yet that did not discourage me.

The State Tax refund took longer than it should have, and I was about to contact them to send it again when one of the staff told me I had a check waiting. It seems they received it weeks before but it was not part of the regular mail call. They never told me. By the time I cashed that check, it was already spent on a new phone and a new bus pass. I had bought myself a little more time.

And so we reach the present. As the days pass, the situation in the shelter does not change. The air conditioning is acting up again, leading me to think that it's a deliberate act in order to save money at the expense of the men in the shelter. The food is as bad as ever.

Now I want to point out that if you are hungry in Raleigh and know where to look, there is free food to be had. But the resources are scattered and when you have no bus pass, you can expend more energy looking for food than you would just waiting for the two meals a day that the shelter serves.

In the current economy, anyone who is homeless and jobless is going to have a hard time, but is that really necessary? Can't something be done to make it easier for a homeless person to live, learn and get out of the situation?

Chapter 2

What needs to change?

In thinking about all the things that could change about the homeless shelters I've been to, the word that pops up first is 'Consistency,' not just between shelters, but in the shelter itself. As it is, most people expect the worst when coming into the shelter now, and are pleasantly surprised when it's not the worst.

Do homeless men in a shelter have the same basic rights as anyone else? Or are shelters just one step above prison? It's a fact that many 'guests' at any shelter are ex-cons. Maybe the shelters are a way of easing their transition. If so those that have never been to prison also have to make that transition.

True, you can leave a shelter, but not after you've checked in, unless you want a bar, or to be kicked out of the program. True, you have a right to free speech, but in the Roanoke Rescue Mission or the Salvation Army shelter, if you wanted to skip church, you could not. I wonder if Jewish or Muslim men have difficulty with that? I'm not a religious person, but I tolerate the large number of Christian organizations that want to come into the SWSC and preach in the dining hall.

True, you get a roof over your head and food to eat, but just because something is free doesn't make it good. The toll on a man's soul is deep in any shelter. It's a burden that's hard to bear. When I walk to the shelter, I have to cross a railroad bridge from downtown Raleigh to the shelter. Every time I cross that bridge, I look over the side and see the railroad ties. Sometimes a train passes underneath. Almost every day when I pass over that bridge the thought goes through my head of jumping off, to end the misery that, admittedly, I brought on myself. Yet I do not jump off. I still have hope that things will change for the better.

So what needs to change? Every city needs a consistent shelter system. A quiet place to sleep and eat and rest so the next day you can continue the job search, or work at your fullest strength, with your mind unclouded with the worry of where you'll sleep that night.

Training programs need to be provided, specifically tuned to the jobs that are being advertised in that city. You have an RTP-style complex near your city? Train for computers. Have a heavy manufacturing base? Train for assembly lines and support work. You can't rely on colleges or even community colleges to provide the workforce you need, because they only offer education and no real experience. The old Biblical adage 'Give a man a fish and he eats for a day; teach a man to fish and he'll eat for life,' works just as well when it comes to computers. It works better when, in addition to teaching, you stand with him while he fishes to make sure he's doing it right and won't need more training.

Don't treat homeless people as second-class citizens. If you see a homeless man holding sign somewhere, asking for money or food, you don't have to give him that money or food, but don't look down at him. Imagine how you'd react if you lost your job and home. Would you want to be treated like that? Of course not.

Churches seem to be the focal point of many charities. Some provide bus passes; some provide food or clothing or even shelter. I'll never understand why Roanoke Rescue Mission treats its 'guests' as they do. Granted the place is loaded with sinners, but does that mean you treat them badly?

Homeless people have a difficult time getting around. Even with cities with buses and subways, it costs money to use them. Some cities provide reduced fare under certain circumstances. But you still need money or know someone willing to donate a pass in order to get around. It shouldn't be hard to stretch the reduced-fare system to a free system for homeless people.

More effort needs to be put out to find homeless people jobs. Perhaps a tax credit to firms that hire homeless people for high-tech positions? Perhaps within each shelter you have the equivalent of Job Link, where job searches can be done on computers.

SWSC had computers the first time I entered it. When I came back in five years alter, those same computers were there, but no one could use them. It seems someone abused the system and SWSC was ordered to not let anyone use them. Rather than hurt everyone else, though, couldn't they simply increase the security on their computers to prevent that from happening again? Maybe train some of the 'guests' in setting up a secure network, rather than shutting down access for everyone because of what one person did.

The lack of health care for the homeless is a problem. Don't get me wrong, if there's an emergency, hospitals will take care of homeless people, but there is no real insurance program for the homeless. Raleigh has what used to be called Horizon, which provided limited health care for the homeless, but needed drugs were rarely free, or were only free once.

Finding adequate, affordable housing is also a problem. Section 8 vouchers have a two-year or more waiting list. And rightfully, women with children come first. Wouldn't it be better to have the homeless have the job they need, with appropriate income, and find a regular apartment or even a house of their own?

The last thing on the list of things to change, should perhaps be the first. There needs to be more respect; between the staff of a shelter and their 'guests;' between guests themselves. Just today, before I started writing, I nearly got into a fight with a man who wanted to squeeze into the bench that starts the food line. I felt uncomfortable about that, not wanting to be packed like a sardine, and he threatened to take me outside and teach me some manners. "I don't care if you're uncomfortable," he said. I told him "That's the problem, you don't care." It ended without a fight, but if I should be beat up before this book goes to print, you know where to look! And this feeling of disrespect is all over the center. People cut into lines, swear a blue streak every other word, push and shove their way onto the bus and have little regard for the 240 other men in the shelter. I've seen one man tell every man in the dorm 'Gimme a dollar. Where's that dollar?' No please, no thank you, not even asking. Just gimme. This, more than anything else, needs to change, in order to bring civilization to the homeless population.

Today I heard the same mantra repeated by several guests. "I hate this place. I gotta get out of here." When so many repeat the same thing, it's time for a change.

In this age of reality TV, the real drama does not come from seeing actors stuck in a house with other actors. It comes from seeing real men struggling to survive day to day in a world designed to make them want to get out.

These are suggestions on how to change things in the here and now. I know resources are limited, budgets are being cut, and social services are being hit hard. Maybe a closer look needs to be taken at what the budget *is* paying for. Can you justify cutting off food and shelter for someone that is homeless just to pay for your pet project?

Perhaps what this country needs is a 'Homeless Bill of Rights.' Or just what follows in the next chapter.

Part II

The Five Points of Hope

Chapter 3

Point 1: Need a Place to Stay?
Stay With Us!

The most basic tenant of Project Five-Star is that everyone who is homeless deserves a high-quality place to stay, with matching high-quality food. The purpose of this is not only to ensure the comfort of our members, but to also train members to build, maintain and cook to the quality of a Five-Star Hotel. How many hotels and restaurants would love to employ people with those skills?

The concept is to build a community of single homeless people, both men and women, though in separate buildings. I suspect there would be more demand for homeless men than women, but the idea is to build 4 dormitory buildings that surround an administrative building that includes classrooms. Surrounding the site itself, will be shops open to the public where the newly trained members can apply their skills. I'd like to arrange for anything bought in those shops to be considered a donation, rather than a purchase.

The dormitory buildings would be 11 floors, 10 floors of rooms, and one floor of offices and classrooms, and rooms for the disabled on the ground floor. Each floor would hold 25 individual rooms, each with a bed, bathroom, and other benefits depending on the level of the member. Two-hundred and fifty members would be in each building.

Each floor would have a meeting area, and its own dining hall, with food provided by the ground-floor kitchen via dumb waiter or elevator. I would expect a steady supply of fresh food available at all times. During non-meal times, that food may consist of fresh fruit and sandwiches. Drinks should be available at all times, including coffee, fresh fruit juices and milk, but carbonated beverages should be available to purchase only. The idea there is to give those with problems with Diabetes free options that won't raise their blood sugar too much.

Each building should be built by members themselves, and should take advantage of the latest in building technology. Each room should be wired for Internet and for WiFi also. I'd like to see solar panels being used, to give the members experience setting those up and also for any Federal tax credits that may come from their use. Computers should run the building and members should build, maintain and program those computers.

The general idea for any aspect of this project is that the money goes as much as physically possible to the members and their accommodations, not to outside organizations. Ultimately, I'd like each center to be self-sufficient, even helping to pay for the next center.

Membership levels would be defined based on how hard the member is willing to work. The levels are: Five-Star, Three-Star and One-Star.

One-Star members would get lowest priority on getting a room. One-Star members are only looking for a place to spend the night, take a shower and a good meal or two. The rooms will have a bed and a bathroom only. There would be no drug/alcohol testing with One-Star members, however drugs and alcohol would not be allowed into the center. One-Star members would be placed in a lottery, and a list would be generated daily, based on the number of rooms available, with the names of those who will be granted a room for a night. I suspect there will not be any room for One-Star members until the center is completely built.

Three-Star members would be considered employees of Project Five-Star. Drug and alcohol testing would be required, with random testing taking place. Three-Star members would either have to be working outside the center or be willing to work and train in one of Project Five-Star's programs, based on space availability. Three-Star members get the same accommodations as One-Star members, but with the addition of a TV and use of a computer. Also in their rooms with be a small washer and dryer. The Three-Star members are considered residents and employees, and they get a stipend of $200/week for putting in 20 hours of work. Three-Star members also have access to the Health/Dental/Vision Clinic. Three-Star members will be asked to leave if their job performance does not meet minimum standards, defined by the supervisor and the Board of Directors.

Five-Star members would have the greatest responsibility, expectations and the greatest rewards. Five-Star members have first choice of programs to join, but must maintain a high quality of standards and workmanship. Five-Star members have the same accommodations and privileges as Three-Star members, with the addition of a project-supplied laptop to bring to class with them. If a Five-Star members fails to maintain the standards as outlined by his supervisor, he will be offered a chance to step down to a Three-Star member, and will be asked to return the laptop.

All Three and Five-Star members have a six-month program of training and on-the-job experience. At the end of the first six months, if a member has not found a job or a place to stay, they can stay in the program, but the stipend will be cut to $140/week for the same number of hours, or whatever the prevailing minimum wage is at the time. After 9 months, the stipend will be cut altogether and they will be considered One-Star members, subject to the same restrictions that other One-Star members face.

It is the responsibility of both the staff and the member to locate suitable employment and housing. Perhaps management can work with a landlord or apartment community to provide housing. Local employers can be contacted to provide entry-level jobs at a living wage for graduates of the program.

The ultimate goal is to get homeless people permanent jobs and permanent housing. Some agencies have no consideration for the comfort of their 'guests,' but I'd rather our members hold their heads up high and say with pride: "I graduated from Project Five-Star. I have the skills you need! Hire me, please!"

Chapter 4

Point 2: Get Healthy!

The current health care system is a myriad of concerns. High costs can be attributed to so many factors, not least to the number of people who can't pay their bill. Equipment costs money to buy and maintain. Experts need to run that equipment Trained doctors and nurses need to see the patients. Malpractice insurance is a necessity.

All this means health care costs money. Project Five-Star would like to provide basic health care services to its members. Basic health care would include checkups, diagnosis and treating of problems, free prescription drugs, simple X-Rays, and referral to a specialist for more complex treatment.

It would also include dental work and vision care. As I stated earlier, my own experiences with dentists leave me in bad shape tooth-wise. I could never afford to get more than every tooth extracted and to wear dentures, something I've seen in the shelter frequently. Dentures are not the best way to handle tooth problems, but they are the cheapest. I'd like the dental clinic at Project Five-Star to use dental implants when necessary. Expensive? Of course, but better for the member in the long run, and overall better for the community. Vision care should work on the same principles

For any work that needs to be provided outside

the clinics, health insurance would be provided for members and out-of-pocket expenses should also be paid for by the center. That should not include simple cosmetic surgery, with the exception of dental implants. I'd like to see agreements reached with local hospitals and doctors to provide care at the lowest rate possible. These people are already homeless and virtually broke. You want to take more?

Mental health services should not be left out of the mix. Though SWSC had fewer mentally ill guests than other shelters I've seen, they still exist and they need care too.

A healthy worker is far more happy and productive than an unhealthy one. In my last full-time job before coming back to the shelter, I suffered from migraines, due in part to stress, that kept me from working to my best potential. Adequate health care would have helped that situation.

Chapter 5

Point 3: Learn a Skill/Use It!

The core of the program, learning a skill will make it possible for our members to find that job and ultimately, find alternative housing.

The six-month training should include Five-Star programs for Chef, Computers (various programs), Landscaping, Automotive Repair, Medical Assistant, Dental Assistant, Construction, Building Maintenance, Security, Administrative, Driving (Chauffeur, Taxi), Banking, Barber/Hairdressing, and Sales.

Three-Star programs should include cooking, food preparation, serving and cleaning. Three-Star members can join in classes for Five-Star programs on a space-available basis, but will have less responsibility.

The programs will be run by experts in their fields: Master Chefs, Computer Gurus, people who have run Five-Star Hotels, Master Mechanics etc., who will be responsible to set the level of expectations for the members, along with the Board of Directors.

The first program to open will be Computers, as part of Phase I, and will be led by me initially, training for A+ certification, Red Hat Linux Administration and Networking. See Chapter 9 for more details. Once sufficient money is raised, the next class would be for the Master Builder program, which will teach members how to use the equipment they will use to build Phase II.

It is my hope to work with local businesses to not only provide jobs, but to help with training as well. Sending a volunteer as a guest lecturer would be nice, but of more importance would be to provide training material to help members pass certification tests and get required licenses.

Once the skill is learned, it's time to use it. Five-Star personnel would be responsible for many of the daily activities of the center. Computer installation and maintenance, setting up a network, driving members where they need to go on project business or looking at housing or interviews, floor monitoring and other security issues, running the stores or restaurants, or plying their trade as a Medical or Dental Assistant, or cooking the food and cleaning the rooms for their fellow members.

And once they have that experience and are ready to take on the world, it's time to look for that job!

Chapter 6

Point 4: Find a Job!

Having looked for a job myself over and over again, I know how frustrating it can get to not be fully prepared for the interview, not be able to get to the interview, or not have the appropriate clothes to wear.

The whole concept of working 20 hours a week within the center is designed to give members time to find a job and look for housing, as well as have some personal time.

Once a member is ready for the next step, all help possible should be given to him or her. A suit and tie for the men, nice dresses for the ladies, and shoes to match. I'd like to bring recruiters to Project Five-Star itself to do interviews, but if that's not possible, Five-Star Chauffeur service will drive members to that all-important interview, and pick them up afterward.

Interview preparation is key to making the right impression the first time. Time should be spent with each member telling them about the company, and having a mock interview so nothing surprises him. Resume preparation should also be provided, and printed by Project Five-Star Publishing.

In a world where there are 10 or more qualified applicants for each position, the best prepared usually walks away with the job.

Project Five-Star would be the last job reference for the employer, and our Human Resources Department should make it clear to the employer what progress the applicant has made and the skills he or she has learned and used.

Once the member lands a job, time to celebrate! I hope we have daily parties as we congratulate each new hire! But our support does not end there. Project Five-Star Chauffeur service will make sure the newly employed member gets to work on time and gets back. The stipend will continue until the member gets his first paycheck, and then it will stop. But he won't stop being a member. We'll support him and begin the process of finding permanent housing!

Chapter 7

Point 5: Find a New Home

The process of finding a new home should be an ongoing one. Many resources for affordable housing are available to any resident of Raleigh. Mostly, it's a matter of having enough money, and having enough time.

Raleigh Housing Authority provides Section 8 vouchers and housing for people 50 or older. The waiting lists, however, are in years. Yet there are programs that will help you find housing when you have a job and you have money. The stipend Project Five-Star will provide is to be used primarily to save for permanent housing and to pay off debts that may prohibit you from finding housing.

Once the Project gets into full-swing, I'd like to form our own Credit Union, and provide interest free loans for down payments on houses for members, to be paid back after the member leaves. Also debt-consolidation loans should be made available. Our bank officers (Five-Star members themselves) can also provide information on mortgages from other banks, as well as general financial information.

With all the resources at the member's disposal, the time to find reasonable, affordable housing should be short. And then it's really time to celebrate!

And after the fun is over, time to move out so the next person-in-need can take over your room!

Chapter 8

Bonus Point: Find a Talent!

You know, living in the shelter, I'm amazed at the level of talent here. I kid about bad singers in the shower, but there are more than a few whose singing inspires me. And I'll bet with a little probing, other hidden talents will show themselves. And maybe Project Five-Star can take those talents, showcase them and make money for both the member and the center.

Love to sing, but never had the resources to record with a band? Have a band but never had the resources to record? Have an idea for a book, but never had time to write it because you were struggling just to survive? Want to take a stab at sculpting or painting? We can provide the resources for that, if you are willing to share any money made from your works with Project Five-Star.

This book is a prime example of that. Though I wrote it, I'm willing to share the royalties with Project Five-Star.

Part of the Project Five-Star website will be dedicated to selling music, books and art made by the members of the center. The profits from selling those items will be divided between the creator and the center, helping both the member and the center and also helping both get noticed.

So part of the Administrative Building will be a

recording studio, with state-of-the-art equipment and someone to train you on it in your spare time. Video equipment and studio space will be made available to promising filmmakers. An art studio and painting a sculpting lessons will also be made available.

I'd like to put together our own video production service, possible part of the skills program, but really, as a way of passing news to members and other interested parties. We can have our own daily newscast, celebrating our triumphs and saying hello and goodbye to members.

Like sports? A section of the center grounds can be used for games and sports. We'll have an exercise area in the Administration Building as well.

I firmly believe that everyone, no matter what your background, has a hidden talent that is waiting to show itself. Maybe you have more than one talent but never had the encouragement to pursue it. Project Five-Star would like to give you that chance.

Part III

The Plan

Chapter 9

Phase I

Phase I of Project Five-Star consists of getting enough money donated to incorporate, get made into a Non-Profit Organization, rent an office, and train 40 people each year on computers to get their A+ certifications, Red Hat Linux Administrator Certifications and Networking Certifications.

The 40 people would be broken into groups of 10, one morning class, one afternoon class, each class lasting six months before the next set of classes starts. I will train the classes myself. Though I don't have those certifications, it would not take me long to get them with the proper funding.

Each class would be broadcast live via webcam over our website, with highlights permanently placed there later. The certifications of each member would be paid for by the Project, but if funding is not available, stipends will not be paid.

I'd like to get at least one van to serve as transportation, but if funding is not available for that, bus passes can be provided to members.

I'd also like to get these members into temporary housing, like a motel, just to get them out of the shelter, however funding for that may not be available.

The idea for Phase I is to show that we mean

business and we're capable of producing certified applicants. Phase I would continue each year until sufficient funding is achieved for Phase II.

Chapter 10

Phase II

Phase II starts when enough funding is achieved to purchase the property where Project Five-Star will reside. At that point a construction expert will be called in, along with an architect to help design the buildings and systems the buildings will use.

The construction expert will determine what equipment needs to be purchased and rented, and then begin the training process of new members on that equipment, working to clear the grounds for the first buildings.

The first buildings to be constructed will be the Administrative Building and the first dormitory. As stated previously, the buildings should be state-of-the art, with solar panels and computer controls. The grounds should be surrounded by a brick wall, to give members brick-laying experience.

Outside of the brick wall, once the first two buildings are constructed, the shops should start to go up. I would like to see a constant stream of construction going on, as well as a constant stream of training.

Once the first two buildings are underway, we begin the process of finding Five and Three-Star members. The Chef program, especially, needs to be started before the buildings are complete, so proper food can be provided once the buildings open. The Chauffeur program should also be started, giving rides to the construction workers and Chefs. The Chefs will provide food for each other as well as the construction workers and Chauffeurs. During this process I'd also like to continue the computer training and have the computer members build and install all the computers and networks used in the buildings.

When the dormitory building is ready, the Chefs, Chauffeurs and Computer experts can move in, and we can begin recruiting for the other programs. North Carolina residents, or residents of whatever state the center is located in, should get first priority. They should be able to prove that they have lived in a shelter and are currently homeless. The programs should have enough people in them so that no one needs to work more than 4 hours in a shift in order to cover all required shifts.

Once the programs are full, if there is space available, members who have a job and just need a temporary place to stay, and access to the resources we provide, will be given a chance to apply.

Each building will need its own cleaning, maintenance, security and food-serving staff. Each floor will have a team of floor monitors who will be the go-to person in case of problems, for supplies and for general monitoring of conditions on the floor. These men would be part of the Five-Star Security team.

Phase II is meant to be the real start of the project, where we pull men off the streets and from overcrowded shelters and bring them into our fold. This is where the money donated to Project Five-Star starts to see fruition, and the hopes of the homeless community will be raised!

Chapter 11

Phase III

When Phase II is complete and the first men move into Project Five-Star, the place will be bustling. Shops will open, services will be provided by highly trained professionals and money will begin pouring in from those services.

At this point construction should begin on the Project Five-Star restaurant, which will provide Raleigh with Five-Star food and drink, cooked, prepared and served by our own Master Chefs. I hope it will be the cornerstone of the services we provide, a way to generate local interest and outside interest as well.

But we'll need more Master Chefs to rotate into the mix, and that means more dormitories; two more dormitories for men, and one for women.

I'd like to see a mini-factory, where members can learn about assembly line techniques and even program robots. I'd like the Raleigh campus to be the cutting edge of technology training.

And once the whole complex is built, the money generated by the services provided can go into building more complexes, in other cities. The cycle goes on. Let's hope in the future we can skip Phase I in other cities and go straight to Phase II and III.

The simple matter is, there are a lot of homeless

people out there in the United States. Far more than most people think, or SWSC wouldn't fill every night. I won't rest until this project catches on and people realize the good that can come from it.

Part IV

Funding

Chapter 12

$1000 from 1000 Companies

I've spent a lot of time trying to work out initial funding for Phase I. If I am to pay the stipend of $200/week for each member, then the first year's budget would have to include $208,000 just for their salaries. I'd need to rent an office, and hire someone experienced with Human Resources to process payroll. My own salary would be limited to $25,000/year, plus room, board and any medical care I need. I'd like to get everyone the medical care they need, and room and board but I'm worried there won't be enough money for that.

So in looking over various ways of generating money, I came up with the proposal of getting donations of $1000 each from 1000 companies. Most companies can spare $1000 for charity, I believe. The challenge then is to find 1000 companies willing to do so.

Writing this book is the first stage of that process. Marketing the book, getting on talk shows and news programs, and getting the concept in front of the people who can make the difference is the next stage.

Selling the book itself will generate some income, both for me and Project Five-Star, but the real money-maker will be to get companies to invest in their potential future employees. I keep hearing that there aren't enough skilled workers who are willing to work cheaply. So companies outsource to countries that have the cheap, skilled labor. Here's an idea: Hire a Project Five-Star graduate, let him or her prove himself while working cheaply. You win, they win, everybody wins. But it won't happen without your donation.

If the goal is met, $1 million will go a long way to getting the project off the ground. We could hire a full-time fund-raiser, maybe even from among the homeless. We can get that office and support staff, and we can start the training that will prove we are capable of supplying the business world with men and women who are ready to perform right out of the blocks.

Helping 40 people a year find jobs by itself is rewarding experience. I'd like to help 500 people or more each year get out of the slums. And if someday we've run out of homeless people, then the real mission will be completed. I don't think that will ever happen, though. Life's just too hard.

Chapter 13

Private Funding

I believe that companies need to be our primary source of initial funding. I'm not going to say no to government checks, but neither am I going to request it. I believe our government has enough problems without Project Five-Star holding out its hand too.

But what about individuals who, out of the kindness of their heart and the generosity of the pocketbook, want to donate? Bless you. You're giving to a program that will give back by taking men and women off the streets and putting them to work so they can give back to their own communities.

The Project Five-Star website will have buttons prominently place for those that want to give online. It will also have information for those wishing to donate by check.

I want to make Project Five-Star as open a program as possible. If you wish to see where our money goes, simply visit our web site and see the videos of our classes, and our budget online.

Chapter 14

Earning Our Own Money

Chapter 8 described a way to find hidden talents within our members. Those talents could raise money for the center in the form of music sales, art sales and book sales (hint, hint). The profits from those sales would be divided equally between the artist and Project Five-Star. The project website would be one outlet for such items, and the one that creates the most profit, but other outlets will be used as well.

We can earn money also from the selling of T-shirts, clothing with the Project Five-Star logo, custom built computer systems and service, web design, food, printing, landscaping, hair styling, and any other services that the center will provide to the public, in order to give our members real world experience.

I'd like to see local concerts on the Project Five-Star grounds, inviting members of the community to see Five-Star talent, as a form of fundraiser.

I expect the money raised to cover at least the operating expenses for each center, making them self-sufficient once Phase III is complete. Any additional income will go toward building a center in the next city, and so on.

I don't expect people to give and keep giving

forever. I'd like the center to take the initial donations, make the best use it can with that money, and then use let the members generate their own money. It's not fair to ask someone to keep giving without getting something back. Project Five-Star will not only give back employees who are ready to work, but give in the form of making other centers in other cities, repeating the process as many times as is necessary to ensure that homeless people in this country have an alternative to sleeping in the streets, or sleeping in a badly run shelter that has its own agenda.

A lot of people may ask why should my money be spent to help homeless bums when you provide services that not everyone can afford?

The answer to that question is two-fold. First, you don't have to give if you don't want to.

Second, they are homeless, and you are not. If you haven't lived in the streets or in a shelter, you cannot be expected to understand the hardship they go through. If you donate time at a shelter or a soup kitchen, Bless you, but you only spend a little time with homeless people. You might look at them and say 'poor dears' and then go to the comfort of your home and not think about what those men and women are going through at the same time you're relaxing.

If you really want to see what it's like, spend one night in a homeless shelter. Just one night will open your eyes to some of the troubles. Staying longer might get you to realize the hopelessness of the current situation.

If, after a week, you still consider homeless bums a nuisance, then please don't give. I want the money that comes into Project Five-Star to be given from the heart, because you want things to change for the better.

My job's not done yet.

Additional information on Project Five-Star:

Website: https://sites.google.com/site/projectfive starraleigh/
(Very much under construction)

Blog: http://projectfivestar.blogspot.com/

Email: projectfivestarraleigh@gmail.com

Donation
link: http://pledgie.com/campaigns/15711

Phone Number (via Google Voice):
(919) 438-1392

Project Five-Star does not have a permanent mailing address at this point. If you wish to donate by mail, please call the number above for more information. Thank you for your support!

Other Books by Michael Harrison Fox

Theater Boy: Part I of the Timmons Chronicles

Kindle Version:
http://www.amazon.com/dp/B004OEKD5U

The Timmons Incident: Part II of the Timmons Chronicles

Kindle Version:
http://www.amazon.com/dp/B004UIGGGA